I0011216

A GUIDE TO SCRUM DEVELOPER

First Edition

Devsena Mishra

(Founder a2zstartup.com)

To my elder sister Gargi Mishra (a renowned geologist) and her husband Mr. Siddharth (technocrat and true entrepreneur) thank you so much for your love and support...

Table of Contents

INTRODUCTION..7

Scrum Overview..8

   What is Scrum?...8

   History 8

   Scrum Framework..9

ARCHITECTURE AND DESIGN 12

   Principles 13

   Agile Modeling Tools...14

TDD-TEST DRIVEN DEVELOPMENT...16

   What is TDD? 16

   Why TDD?...17

   TDD/ATDD and BDD...17

EXTREME PROGRAMMING (XP) PRACTICES 19

   User stories...19

   Small releases...20

   Metaphor 20

   Collective ownership 20

   Coding standard 20

   Simple design...20

   Refactoring...20

   Testing 20

   Pair programming 21

   Continuous integration..21

   40-hour workweek 21

   On-site customer 22

REFACTORING 23

   Refactoring- When?..23

     SOME COMMON BAD SMELLS AND REFACTORING TECHNIQUES TO REMOVE THEM23

Refactoring – How? 26

CONTINUOUS INTEGRATION 34

Continuous Deployment 34

Principals of CI 35

Advantages of CI 36

Best Practices for Team 37

TOOLS for AGILE DEVELOPMENT 39

TDD Toolkit... 39

CI Toolkit... 40

A Brief Introduction to BDD 43

And now some Tools for Agile project management 45

WATERFALL TO AGILE 47

SCRUM Versus SAFe.. 49

CURRENT STATE of AGILE/SCRUM ACCEPTANCE.. 51

DevOps 52

References 56

6

CHAPTER 1

INTRODUCTION

Brief and simple was the goal in my mind when I decided to write a book on Scrum Developer. I observed that a number of good books and articles are available on Scrum/Agile development practices but these pieces of information are scattered here and there and if someone needs a quick review and interested in only a basic understanding then assembling this information becomes a tough task…this book is intended to simplify this task. Officially, Certified Scrum Developer is one who has attended a formal training and cleared a technical skills assessment, agenda of these trainings broadly covers working understanding of Scrum principles and Agile engineering practices. Today when most of the organizations are experimenting with Agile/Scrum methodology, it becomes necessary for an IT Professional to have some familiarity with Agile Engineering practices. The targeted audiences of this book are: Software developers (whether working in agile or waterfall model), Managers (who needs basic understanding of techniques and jargons of agile) and anyone who is a part of Agile project or going to join an agile project and looking for a basic understanding of agile engineering practices…I tried to keep the things as simple and straight as possible because as a reader, I always seek simple and to the point source of knowledge.

In the chapter 2 I have given a brief introduction to Scrum Framework, understanding of Scrum framework helps and sets a context of agile project culture in the mind of reader. Chapter 3 is about Agile Architecture and Design, this chapter will help in understanding agile architecture approach and principals of Agile Modeling. Chapter 4 to Chapter 7 covers the Agile Engineering practices, on core practices like TDD, Refactoring and Continuous Integration there is a separate chapter for each and summary of rest of the XP practices is provided in a separate chapter (Chapter 5). Chapter 8 covers brief information about tools/frameworks that one needs in an agile project because speed and accuracy is the main element of agile environment and for this we need to get rid of manual error prone approach of development and should adopt automation (at maximum level possible). Last four chapters are a collection of my previously published articles, which I included in this book to give readers some thoughts on latest trends and development in the field of Scrum/Agile…

I have learned different methodologies/frameworks (Scrum/Agile, PMP, PRINCE2, Lean, Six Sigma) and I observed that all these methodologies/framework are for the betterment and quality of the process and we need to ensure that these should not turn into a hurdle for the team and project.

CHAPTER 2

Scrum Overview

This chapter is a brief introduction to Scrum framework: Scrum definition, History of Scrum, the Scrum team, Scrum events, Scrum Artifacts and definition of "Done".

What is Scrum?

Scrum is a framework for managing software development projects in an agile way, it is easy to understand, adopt and use. Earlier there were different frameworks in use like waterfall, prototyping, iterative and incremental development, spiral, rapid application development etc. but there is no doubt that Scrum is popular of them all.

History:

Jeff Sutherland and Ken Schwaber conceived the Scrum process in the early 90's. They codified Scrum in 1995 in order to present it at the Oopsla conference in Austin, Texas (US) and published the paper "SCRUM Software Development Process". Ken and Jeff inherited the name 'Scrum' from the 1986 groundbreaking paper 'The New Product Development Game' by Takeuchi and Nonaka, two acknowledged management thinkers. With the term 'Scrum' Nonaka and Takeuchi referred to the game of rugby to stress the importance of teams and some analogies between a team sports like rugby and being successful in the game of new product development. The research described in their paper showed that outstanding performance in the development of new, complex products is achieved when teams, as small and self-organizing units of people, are fed with objectives, not with tasks. The best teams are those that are given direction within which they have room to devise their own tactics on how to best head towards their joint objective. Teams require autonomy to achieve excellence. The Scrum framework for software development implements the principles described in this paper for developing and sustaining complex software products. While in the process of developing and using early versions of Scrum, Ken asked Professor Babatunde A. Ogunnaike Tunde, a famous process control research engineer, to look at software development processes. Tunde investigated several commercial software-development methodologies to conclude that the waterfall and predictive process is not a good fit for the work of software development. He confirmed the empirical approach of Scrum to be the preferred process [1].

In February 2001, Jeff and Ken were amongst the 17 software development leaders creating the Manifesto for Agile Software Development. Following the Agile Manifesto, the Agile Alliance was founded with Ken Schwaber being its first chairman. In 2001, much inspired by Kent Beck, Ken Schwaber co-authored the first book on Scrum with Mike Beedle "Agile Software Development with Scrum". In 2002, Ken Schwaber founded the Scrum Alliance with Mike Cohn and Esther Derby, with Ken chairing the organization. In the years to follow the highly successful Certified Scrum Master programs and its derivatives were created and launched. In 2006, Jeff Sutherland created his own company, Scrum.inc, while continuing to offer and teach the Certified Scrum courses. Ken left the Scrum Alliance in the fall of 2009, and founded Scrum.org to further improve the quality and effectiveness of Scrum, mainly through the Professional Scrum series. With the first publication of the Scrum Guide in 2010, and its incremental updates in 2011 and 2013, Jeff and Ken established the globally recognized body of knowledge of Scrum [1].

Scrum Framework

As Mike Cohn (founder moutaingoatsoftware.com) has defined Scrum is a project management framework that is applicable to any project with aggressive deadlines, complex requirements and a degree of uniqueness. In Scrum, projects move forward via a series of iterations called sprints. Each sprint is typically two to four weeks long [2].

A quick review of Scrum framework:

- A product owner (PO) creates a prioritized list of features called product backlog.
- During sprint planning meeting, the team pulls some items from the top of product backlog and creates a sprint backlog, and discuss how to implement those pieces in this upcoming sprint.
- The team works in time boxed iteration called—sprint (usually two to four weeks long), team meets each day to assess its progress this meeting is called daily Scrum, a time boxed 15 min discussion on what is done, what is on way, and if there is any hurdle?
- Scrum Master ensures that team remains focused on its goal.
- At the end of the sprint, the work should be potentially shippable.
- The sprint ends with a sprint review and retrospective.
- As the next sprint begins, the team will gather for sprint planning meeting and begins working again.

Let's take a look at some important concepts of Scrum:

Scrum team: Scrum team consists of Product Owner, Scrum Master and the Development team. A scrum team should be cross functional and should build up a culture of self organization. A typical scrum team has between five and nine people, but Scrum projects can scale into teams of teams. There exists a technique called scrums of scrums in Scrum framework that is used to scale Scrum up to large groups for big enterprise projects. In the year 2011 Mr. Dean Leffingwell introduced a new framework called "SAFe (Scaled Agile Framework)", in a very short duration this framework has gained good popularity. The proponents of SAFe claim that it is required for large enterprise projects☺ in the chapter Scrum V/S SAFe I have discussed all these aspects in detail.

Product owner: The product owner (PO) represents users and customers. PO is responsible for creating and maintaining product backlog, if team has some concern/doubt related to a requirement/product feature they can clarify it with PO.

Scrum Master: The Scrum Master plays the role of a mentor/facilitator/coach. SM is responsible for ensuring that the team remains productive and on track.

Scrum Events:

Sprint planning meeting: At the beginning of each sprint, team gather to plan upcoming sprint, this is called a sprint planning meeting. In this meeting the product owner presents some items from the product backlog to the team. The Scrum team discusses and selects the work they can complete and put their selection in another list called sprint backlog, this list specifically contains those items that team has committed to complete in the upcoming sprint.

Daily Scrum: Each day during the sprint, a brief 15 minutes time boxed meeting called daily scrum is conducted. This meeting helps set the context for each day's work and helps the team stay on track. All team members should attend the daily scrum (for distributed team teleconferencing will work).

Sprint review meeting: At the end of each sprint, the team demonstrates the completed functionality at a sprint review meeting, during which, the team shows what they have accomplished during the sprint. Typically, this takes the form of a demonstration of the new features, but in an informal way; for example, PowerPoint slides are not allowed. The meeting must not become a task in itself nor a distraction from the process [2].

Sprint retrospective: Also at the end of each sprint, the team conducts a sprint retrospective, which is a meeting during which the team (including its Scrum Master and product owner) discusses that how well Scrum is working for them and what changes they may wish to make for improvement [2].

Scrum Artifacts:

Product backlog: The product backlog is a prioritized features list containing every desired feature or change to the product. Note: The term "backlog" can get confusing because it's used for two different things. To clarify, the product backlog is a list of desired features for the product. The sprint backlog is a list of tasks to be completed in a sprint.

Sprint backlog: During sprint planning meeting when team conducts a discussion about what will go in next sprint that resulted in a list called Sprint Backlog. Most teams also estimate how many hours each task will take someone on the team to complete. It is important that the team selects the items and size of the sprint backlog. In the simplest possible way it is maintained in an excel sheet but team can also use some specialized software product or some defect tracking tool.

Increment: The Increment or potentially shippable increment is the sum of all the product backlog items completed during a sprint and all previous sprints. At the end of a sprint, the increment must be complete, according to Scrum definition of Done and in a usable condition regardless of whether the product owner decides to actually release [3].

Definition of "Done": Each team decides it own definition of done (like acceptance criteria), it is a criteria that must be met before considering a product backlog item or an increment to be complete or "done". Mike Cohn has described that a typical DoD would be something similar to: The code is well written. (That is, we're happy with it and don't feel like it immediately needs to be rewritten.) The code is checked in. (Kind of an "of course" statement, but still worth calling out.) The code was either pair programmed or peer reviewed. The code comes with tests at all appropriate levels. (That is, unit, service and user interface).

The feature the code implements has been documented in any end-user documentation such as manuals or help systems [4].

Some teams can benefit from having multiple definitions of "Done" at different levels. It depends on their project's nature, complexity and approach because when we are defining "Done" we need to remember that we are making a decision about a feature/product and what is important is that there exist a shared understanding among team members.

To conclude I would say Scrum is a simple and easy to adapt framework, some people claim that its acceptance need a huge culture or mindset change, on that I would say nature of software development domain is volatile and professionals who belongs to this domain have a natural tendency of learning and adapting to new things...this whole debate of mindset or culture change is a part of its branding, and that is good ☺

CHAPTER 3

ARCHITECTURE AND DESIGN

This chapter will give you an overview of architecture and design aspect of Scrum: how concept of design is different in Scrum from earlier methodologies, agile architecture principals and main features of agile modeling.

Design and architecture is crucial for the success of any project, a good design can save time, resources and money (often spend in maintains and redundant tasks), here we will not discuss what is good design and bad design rather we will try to understand how to approach architecture and design as a member of Scrum team.

It is always nice to make all design decisions upfront, but doing so is almost impossible, therefore Scrum favors **incremental, just in time approach** to design. Scrum design approach is considered as **intentional yet emergent**, to put in simple words design in Scrum project is intentional because it is natural that team chooses items from product backlog with some design intention (conscious decision making), so there exist some intentional architecture, and design is emergent because there is no up-front analysis or design phase exist as all these activities happens repeatedly in sprints.

Agile Architecture Principals:

Let's take a look at the **seven principles of Agile architecture** (as described by Mr. Dean Leffingwell) [5]:

Principle #1- Design emerges, Architecture is collaboration.

Principle #2 -The bigger the system, the longer the runway

Principle #3- Build the simplest architecture that can possibly work

Principle #4 -When in doubt, code or model it out.

Principle #5- They build it, they test it

Principle #6- There is no monopoly on innovation

Principle #7- Implement architectural flow

A detail explanation of all these principles is provided in a full whitepaper at: http://www.scaledagileframework.com/agile-architecture/ -

The agile teams typically need someone as "Architecture Owner", just like the product owner is responsible for the team's requirements, the architecture owner is responsible for the team's architecture. Architecture owners take an approach which is collaborative and evolutionary, not command-and-control and certainly not serial [6].

Agile Modeling: Agile Modeling is a way of modeling software product by keeping certain values, principles and practices in mind. In the book "Agile Modeling" Scott W. Ambler has given a good explanation of values, principles and practices for modeling software that can be applied on a software development project [7].

Values: The values of AM are communication, simplicity, feedback, courage and humility. For the success of a software model it is necessary that project stakeholders communicate effectively, strive to develop simplest solution possible, accept feedback early to make desired improvements, should have courage to make and stick to design decisions so that quality of the design should not compromise also an agile modeler should have humbleness to admit that he/she may not know everything and opinions of others can add value to project.

Principles: Scott has organized AM principles into two parts: core principles and supplementary principles:

Core Principles	Supplementary Principles
Assume Simplicity	Content is More Important Than Representation
Embrace Change	
	Open and Honest Communication
Enabling the Next Effort is Your Secondary Goal	
Incremental Change	
Maximize Stakeholder ROI	
Model With a Purpose	
Multiple Models	
Quality Work	
Rapid Feedback	
Working Software Is Your Primary Goal	
Travel Light	

Source: http://www.agilemodeling.com

These principles talked about **"assuming simplicity"** because simplest solution is the best solution and **"embracing change"** because one needs to understand that requirements evolve over time. People's understanding of the requirements change over time. Project stakeholders can change as your project moves forward, new people are added and existing ones can leave. Project stakeholders can change their viewpoints as well, potentially changing the goals and success criteria for your effort. Also an agile modeler should know why he/she is working on a particular model that is principal **"model with a purpose"**, the first step is to identify a valid purpose for creating a model and the audience for that model, then based on that purpose and audience develop it to the point where it is both sufficiently accurate and sufficiently detailed. The principle **"enabling next effort is your secondary goal"** is crucial too, as Alistair Cockburn has described when you are playing the software development game your secondary goal is to setup to play the next game. Your next effort may be the development of the next major release of your system or it may simply be the operations and support of the current version you are building. To enable it you will not only want to develop quality software but also create just enough documentation and supporting materials so that the people playing the next game can be effective [7]. Scott has emphasized that **one should travel as light as possible** that is do not burden yourself with too much models because each model you keep will bring overhead of maintenance of its documentation. Therefore traveling light in the context of AM means one should spend time on those models and documents that are actually going to fulfill your purpose. But remember traveling too light or too heavy both are undesired.

Practices: Scott (in his book Agile Modeling) has described certain practices that an agile modeler should adopt like **creating several models in parallel, applying the right artifacts** for the situation and **iterating to another artifact** to continue moving forward at a steady pace. **Modeling in small increments** and not attempting to create the magical "all encompassing model" from your ivory tower are crucial for the success of an agile modeler. Because models are only abstract representations of software, abstractions that may not be accurate, you should strive to **prove it with code** to show that your ideas actually work in practice and not just in theory. **Active stakeholder participation** is critical to the success of your modeling efforts because your project stakeholders know what they want and can provide you with the feedback that you require. The principle of assume simplicity is a supported by the practices of **creating simple content** by focusing only on the aspects that you need to model and not attempting to creating a highly detailed model, **depicting models simply** via use of simple notations, and **using the simplest tools** to create your models. You travel light by **single sourcing information, discarding temporary models and updating models only when it hurts** [7]. For the implementation of Agile Modeling principals, these practices are required because practices are practical version of principals.

Agile Modeling Tools:

It is always advisable to use the simplest tool possible, because simple tools are easy to use, learn and share. Although some projects require use of complex tools but unnecessary use of complex tools for modeling should be avoided. Simple tool like pencil, paper and whiteboard in most of the cases are sufficient to discuss and design a good model.

What is important is that while designing a software model, one should have some design goals in mind like a design should be simple, explicit, cohesive, decoupled and isolated. XP practices like TDD, refactoring, automated testing, continuous integration, pair programming, collective ownership, quick design sessions, and code/design reviews etc. are helpful for a good design.

To conclude I would say Agile Architecture and Design approach is customer and quality focused. This shift from traditional design practice to agile design practice can make designers and other team members uncomfortable (in the initial stage) but once they will realize the importance of rapid feedback and collaboration they will enjoy it. At the end a good design to some extent depends on our desire/ability to keep code clear and simple, continuous refactoring, knowledge of pattern and the ability of designing with an eye to future demands.

CHAPTER 4

TDD-TEST DRIVEN DEVELOPMENT

Test driven development (TDD) is a technique of driving design of software using automated unit tests. This chapter will cover typical question which comes in the mind of a developer like what is TDD, why TDD, TDD vs Test First Design, the difference between TDD/ATDD and BDD and we will also take a look at the critics of TDD, because there is a huge debate going on in the favor and opposition of TDD ("TDD is dead" controversy).

What is TDD?
TDD (Test Driven Development) is the practice of creating test, before coding or any detailed design. Thinking about test before code is not natural for a developer because developers are tend to jump to solutions (sometimes before understanding the problem in detail ☺), but there is no doubt that when we think about test scenarios before code, we cover some more hidden aspects of requirement and that resulted in a working, tested and quality code.

TDD approach talks about a cycle to be followed repeatedly and that is: RED-> GREEN-> and CLEAN

Here RED means writing a failing test (because functionality which it is testing not yet exist), then writing the chunk of code to satisfy the test, now test should pass (the GREEN phase), and after this CLEAN the code, that is Refactor the code to make it well structured.

Martin fowler has given two benefits of this approach in his blog: most obviously it's a way to get SelfTestingCode, since you can only write some functional code in response to making a test pass. The second benefit is that thinking about the test first forces you to think about the interface to the code first. This focus on interface and how you use a class helps you separate interface from implementation [8].

To some people Test First Development and Test Driven Development seems confusing and both look almost same, and they are…in their approach, but I would say TDD is special case of Test First Development in which we also focus on a cleaner design by refactoring the code repeatedly and this single difference adds the element of Continuous Design.

Why TDD?

Here I would put three reasons- one is writing and running unit tests helps improve your code, because unit test is using our application code, second is thorough unit testing (an optimal number of test coverage) brings confidence and third I believe is that thinking about test before code and refactoring it frequently is a good practice to be followed, however one can choose to make this practice a habit or not but if your mind is calm and everything is on track then why not do it perfectly and follow all good practices.

TDD/ATDD and BDD

ATDD stands for acceptance test driven development, in this practice we create automated acceptance tests before code, it talks about developer, tester and business customer collaboration. ATDD encompasses many of the same practices as Specification by Example, Behavior Driven Development (BDD), Example-Driven Development (EDD), and Story Test-Driven Development (SDD). A good TDD is depends on acceptance test too, so we can say that:

TDD = acceptance test+ xUnit

BDD- Behavior driven development is related more with TDD. Although BDD is principally an idea about how software development should be managed by both- business interests and technical insight, the practice of BDD does assume the use of specialized software tools (automation tools) to support the development process [9].

TDD critics and the "TDD is dead" controversy

David Heinemeier Hansson (Ruby on Rails author and founder of Basecamp) has written two posts "TDD is Dead- Long Live Testing" and "Test Induced Design Damage" the points which he made (as summarized by Brian Oken) are:

--Lots of developers that push TDD make you feel like your code is dirty if you are not using TDD.

--Driving your design from unit tests is not a good idea.

--The TDD notion of "tests must be fast" is shortsighted.

--The faith in TDD can lead to completely forgetting about system testing.

--The focus on the unit and the unit only doesn't help with producing a great system.

--100% coverage is silly

--Programmers want software to be a science, but it isn't. It's more like creative writing.

--Good software isn't like engineering.

--It's like writing. Clear concise writing is better than convoluted writing.

--Clarity is good. So good that clarity should be the number one goal, not test coverage or test speed.

--Being a good developer is as hard as becoming a good writer.

--Just like writing, the way to become a good programmer is to write a lot of software, read a lot of software, aim for clarity [10] [11].

In the month of May'2014 a thorough discussion happened between Kent Beck, David Heinemeier Hansson, and Martin Fowler on the topic of Test-Driven Development (TDD) and its impact upon software design, in that discussion various conflict points like confidence and TDD, test induced design damage, costs associated with too much testing and so on were discussed. You can read that full discussion at: http://martinfowler.com/articles/is-tdd-dead/

Such arguments (both in favor or opposition) are natural because this approach of thinking about Test before code causes some discomfort and not everyone will be OK with this, and it may not be ideal in some scenarios too. The decision to enable TDD practice in a project depends on a number of factors like complexity of requirements/design, time and experience constraint of developers, existence of legacy code, level of coupling in system etc.

I believe that any kind of practices be it applying design patterns, agile principles, XP practices including TDD, that brings quality in code is good but at the same time a team should be mature enough to take informed decisions because all these things (methodologies/techniques) exist for the product we suppose to deliver, hence one should always keep product in center and plan the things around.

CHAPTER 5

EXTREME PROGRAMMING (XP) PRACTICES

In this chapter I'll give you a brief overview of all twelve practices of Extreme Programming (XP). XP is a software development methodology primarily developed by Kent Beck, it is one of the first agile methods. Some of the popular XP practices are: Continuous Integration, Refactoring, Test Driven Development and Agile Planning.

Now let's take a look:

User stories: User story is a short and simple high level requirement artifact, a typical user story format is: As a <user>, I want to <some goal> so that <some goal>

The customer defines the desired features for the new application and describes each feature's business value and priority. In an agile project user stories helps and affect Scheduling and Estimating. User stories are often written on index cards or sticky notes, the idea is to use simplest tool possible. A good user story should have the property of I.N.V.E.S.T (it's a mnemonic created by Bill Wake as a reminder of the characteristics of a good quality user story) where:

I- Independent-The user story should be self-contained, in a way that there is no inherent dependency on another user story.

N- Negotiable- User stories, up until they are part of an iteration, can always be changed and rewritten.

V- Valuable- A user story must deliver value to the end user.

E- Estimatable- You must always be able to estimate the size of a user story.

S- Small- User stories should not be so big as to become impossible to plan/task/prioritize with a certain level of certainty.

T- Testable- The user story or its related description must provide the necessary information to make test development possible [12].

Who writes user story- Anyone from the team can write it, Product Owner responsible for ensuring that a backlog of user stories should exist but any team member can write it (after discussing with customer).

Before we start implementing user stories, we needs to add details into it- typically we add details in a user story either - during requirement/model storming with customer, during iteration planning or during implementation. Details can be added by- breaking down the user story into multiple smaller user stories and by adding Condition of Satisfaction (high level acceptance criteria).

The difference between User story and Use case is that use case organize requirement into a narrative of how user relate to or use the system while user story breaks those requirement into smaller chunks which is useful for planning process. A user story should have all three elements- Card, Conversation and Confirmation.

Small releases: XP focuses on developing and delivering the application in a series of small, frequently updated versions. As each new requirement is added, complete the system and re-release. Working in small releases brings fast feedback as feedback cycle also get reduces because with each small release customer share its feedback so that any kind of issue can get sort out in the next release.

Metaphor (standardized naming schemes): XP naming conventions specify how developers name their methods, classes, variables, events and parameters. The purpose is that a name should make it easy to guess about the functionality, one should name code items in way that name describes the whole purpose. These standardized naming schemes are a part of coding standard that team members should follow and it brings consistency in the code.

Collective ownership: As it is clear from the name, this practice state that any member of the team can change any piece of code in the system at anytime. Ownership brings responsibility and saves a lot of time because now no one needs to wait for anyone, if you feel you can work on it and improve it, you should…code is reviewed and updated by everyone on the team and it brings shared knowledge of code, reduces the risk that absence of anyone can stall or slow the work, improves the overall design because now it is under the scrutiny of many eyes and makes individual to feel responsible for the quality of the whole.

Coding standard: This practice brings a consistent style in code, irrespective of who writes it, because it talk about some standards for formatting, code structure, naming conventions, error handling and comments that all team members should follow. This allows for rapid code sharing and reduces the learning curve for other developers.

Simple design: This practice says that while coding we should always try the simplest thing that work, because the best design is the easiest one that works. A correct design for an XP system is one that runs all the unit and functional tests, one that is clear, expressive and consistent, duplicates no behavior or configuration (DRY- Do not Repeat Yourself) and uses minimal methods, classes and modules.

Refactoring: XP says that when you see something, anywhere in the code, that could be made clearer or simpler or something that needs to be refactored for you to make the next change you want to make, you should change it right away. The idea is that starting with anything that works and refactoring it as problems arise will produce well-designed code without the need for lengthy design at the start of the project. But it is important that team members should have a shared understanding of the application and should continuously revise the system without duplicating the code.

Testing: TDD – Test Driven Development is originated out of the Test First Approach of XP, which says that one should write the tests first and then develop the code to meet the requirements of the test. This allows for a clean/simple application and brings confidence in system, by flushing out problems before they get lost in a large application. This approach ensures that every piece of code that is written is tested before moving on to the next feature.

Pair programming: Programming is done in pair, when two people work together on the same functionality (sitting side by side), it brings quality in code, because when one person is coding, the other person is scanning his work…this practice needs coding standards to be followed for uniformity. The pair not just writes code, they suppose to write tests as well. This kind of collaboration has many soft benefits too, and managers can see this as an opportunity for team spirit building. (an ideal pair programming session should not stretch more than 3 hours).

Martin Fowler (in his article "PairProgrammingMisconceptions") has shared some interesting points [13]:

You have to do pair programming if you're doing an agile process- it is not right because pair programming belongs to XP not agile, it is not even mentioned in the Agile Manifesto…agile only prescribes some values and principles and it is not necessary that all agile projects should follow XP practices.

Extreme Programming forces you to do Pair-Programming- A XP team adopt all these practices day by day and XP does not forces pair programming or any other practice on a team, a team should try and watch whether a practice works for them or not.

I don't need to try pairing because I know I won't like it- It's a social skill and some people may take time to get comfortable with it…but first they have to try it.

Pair-Programming halves the productivity of developers- On this Martin has said "Of course, since we Cannot Measure Productivity we can't know for sure. My view is that you should try it and the team should reflect on whether they feel they are more effective with pairing than without".

Continuous integration: It talks about merging all developer working copies to a Master/Trunk/Mainline branch frequently; Martin Fowler has given a comprehensive definition of CI: Continuous Integration is a software development practice where members of a team integrate their work frequently, usually each person integrates at least daily - leading to multiple integrations per day. Each integration is verified by an automated build (including test) to detect integration errors as quickly as possible [14].

In a typical CI workflow, Developer checks in code to development branch, Continuous Integration Server picks up the change, performs Unit Tests, votes on the Merge to Staging environment based on test results, if successful deploys it to Staging Environment, QA tests the Environment, if passed, they vote to move to Production, Continuous Integration server picks this up again and determines if it is ok to merge into Production, if successful, it will deploy to Production environment. This process varies slightly based on needs, requirements and approaches [15].

40-hour workweek: The main purpose of all the practices of XP (or any other methodology) is to bring quality in code. Overtime working and stressed teams cannot deliver quality product, one need to learn how to complete the task within shift…and it is seen that a good weekend break boost the energy and satisfaction level of individuals (which is required for quality work).

On-site customer: In an agile project where we are working in small cycles and our iterations are depends on the direct feedback, it is required that the customer (or customer proxy) is available to discuss things out. The customer must be available at all times to set priorities, deliver and establish requirements, and answer questions.

In his famous book Kent Beck has shared 15 XP principles too, these are: Rapid Feedback, Assume Simplicity, Incremental Change, Embracing Change, Quality Work, Teach Learning, Small Initial Investment, Play to Win, Concrete Experiments, Open, honest Communication, Work with people's instincts - not against them, Accepted Responsibility, Local Adaptation, Travel Light, and Honest Measurement.

For more detail I suggest you to read Kent Beck's book- **Extreme Programming Explained: Embrace Change,** it's a detailed research on XP and will give more insights about extreme programming practices.

CHAPTER 6

REFACTORING

Refactoring is a change made to the internal structure of software to make it easier to understand and cheaper to modify without changing its observable behavior [16]. In this chapter we will see the important elements of refactoring, when and how to perform refactoring and the common refactoring techniques.

With the use of modern IDEs in development, the techniques of refactoring become a part of routine coding practices. Refactoring brings clarity in the code and educated/planned use of refactoring can help programmer to a great extent. Refactoring cleans up the code and minimizes the chances of bugs and improves the design of the software.

Refactoring- When?
IDEs that we use for development includes the inbuilt support for Refactoring, the need is to understand which technique will solve what kind of problem, but before that one should be aware about the pain points of a codebase typically called "bad smells" in a code because before understanding how to perform refactoring one need to know the when part, because refactoring is applicable when there are some bad smells in the code....

SOME COMMON BAD SMELLS AND REFACTORING TECHNIQUES TO REMOVE THEM: (These smells are mentioned in Martin Fowler's book: Refactoring-Improving the Design of Existing Code [16])

DUPLICATE CODE: If same code structure appears in more than one location then we should try to find a way to unify that because duplicate code is prone to bugs, difficult to maintain and enhance.

Typical scenarios are:

1. Duplicate code in 1 or more methods of same class

    Refactoring-Extract Method (6)

2. Duplicate Code in multiple sibling subclasses.

    Refactoring- Extract method (6) to remove duplication and then **pull up method (17).**

    If code is similar not same then use **extract method (6)** to unify similar part and then we can apply **Form Template Method (9).**

If there is more than one method that performs the same thing but their algorithms are different, then select simple/clearer of them and use **Substitute Algorithm (24)**.

3. Duplicate code in unrelated classes

   Refactoring- Extract Class (4) and use the new component in place of code where it make sense.

LONG METHOD: A method is considered long if it is performing multiple tasks and as a result there is a need to put comments to describe sections and also if it is taking multiple parameters. A long method is difficult to read/modify/reuse and unit test and also it is prone to bugs.

Refactoring- Most of the time we apply **Extract Method (6)** to decompose long methods, but when we try extract method we get long list of parameters and temporary variables as parameters to the extracted method. To eliminate temps we can use **Replace Temp with query (23)** and to reduce the long lists of parameters we can use **Introduce parameter Object (13)** and **Preserve whole object (16)**.

Even after trying above refactoring if still too many temps and parameters are left then we can apply **Replace Method with Method Object (21)**.

To decompose conditional loop we can use **Decompose Conditional (2)** and for loops use **extract the loop (8)** and replace the code with loop into its own method.

LARGE CLASS: A class is considered large if it is performing multiple things (to avoid this SRP- Single Responsibility Principal should be followed) and if it has too many Instances (class) variables that lead to duplicate code. First of all, such a class is a direct violation of SRP design principle that says a class should have only single responsibility to handle and second it is also difficult to change the behavior of such class if any such requirement comes and lastly such class is difficult to unit test as well.

Refactoring- Extract Class (4) or **Extract subclass (7)** depends on the scenario and further **Extract Interface (5)** can be applied.

If it's a GUI class then we need to move data and behavior separately this may require keeping some common data in both location in such case we can apply **Duplicate Observed Data (3)**.

LONG PARAMETER LIST: Long parameter list are hard to understand, since we change them whenever we need more data, these lists become inconsistent and difficult to use. One way to shorten the parameter list is to pass the object as a parameter but if only doing does not solve our purpose then we can use **Replace parameter with method (22)**, main objective of this refactoring is that if a method can get a value that is passed in as a parameter by another means then it should. It is for those situations when we are calling a method, storing its return value in temp field and then passing this field to another method as a parameter:

int somevalue = getSomeValue();

methodUsingSomeValue(somevalue);

Now why can't we make this call to getSomeValue() inside the body of the method methodUsingSomeValue() and remove its parameter, we can...then remove the parameter and let the receiver method (methodUsingSomeValue()) invoke the method (getSomeValue()).

We can also use **Preserve Whole Object (16)** if we are getting several values from an object and passing these values as a parameter in a method call, then instead of doing this we can pass the whole object. Another refactoring for long parameter lists is **Introduce Parameter Object (13)** it is useful when we have a set of parameter which we are passing again and again as one group, then we can replace this group of parameters with an object.

Such refactoring techniques are not applicable in all cases, especially when we do not want to introduce dependency between called object and larger object, in such situations it is logical to pass data as a parameter.

DIVERGENT CHANGE: Divergent change occurs when one class is regularly changed in different ways for different reasons, if it is so (which is very natural) then it's time to divide the class into separate objects so that each object is changed only as a result of one kind of change. To refactor this we need to identify everything that changed for a particular cause and then we can use **Extract Class (4)** to put that all together. If you found an opposite situation (**Shotgun Surgery**) that is for every new change you have to alter a lot of different classes then use **Move Method (15)** and **Move Field (14)** to put all changes into a single class.

Divergent change is one class that suffers many kinds of changes, and shotgun surgery is one change that alters many classes. Either way you want to arrange things so that, ideally, there is a one-to-one link between common changes and classes [16].

LAZY CLASS AND SPECULATIVE GENERALITY: A lazy class is one that exist without much functionality, it may be added for some reasons that were planned but not implemented or may be it reduces as a result of refactoring, whatever may be the reason if it is not worth to maintain it then we should remove it as early as possible. Speculative Generality name is suggested by Brian Foote for a smell which occur when we have created some abstract class (may be with few implementation) and in reality this class is not doing much and no other part is using it except some test cases, if some subclasses are implemented out of it then to clean this up we can use **Collapse Hierarchy (1)** and unnecessary delegation can be removed with **Inline Class (11).**

Not only classes, we need to find those methods too which are not using anywhere except in test classes and also those which are having unused parameter list. In these cases it is better to delete such methods (or their parameters using **Remove Parameter (19)**) and classes and clean-up the code.

TEMPORARY FIELD: Sometime we find that a class is containing a lot of optional fields, these instance variables are set in only certain situations, but their presence makes the code hard to understand and without understanding the logic of code it is difficult to make any change.

A number of temporary fields also crop up in a situation when an algorithm requires lots of variables and instead of passing a long parameter list we are using fields inside method (called) body…to clean up the code in these situations we can use **Extract Class (4)** for these variables and methods that need them.

MESSAGE CHAIN AND MIDDLE MAN: We have often seen message chains when multiple getXYZ() are called in the client code to get the required information, that creates a long list of getXYZ() methods, this creates a dependency between client code and structure of server code…and any change to this structure (delegate object) will cause the client to change too. And not only this, here we are also exposing our server's domain structure to client. (While we have learned in OOPs that encapsulation is one of the main features of OO programming and that is –hiding internal details from the rest of the world).

One way to fix this is to use **Hide Delegate (10)** refactoring, hide delegate simply put a delegating method on the server code (here server means the code which client is accessing), which hides the delegate object, but this move often turns server object into a middle man. Middle Man is a class which is delegating half of its client calls to another class and when it becomes too much confusing we need to perform **Remove Middle Man (18),** which is inverse of Hide Delegate, here client calls the delegate object directly.

To remove middle man we need to create an accessor for the delegate, and for each client call to delegating method on the server, remove the delegating method and replace the client call with this call to accessor of delegate, for this we can use **Inline Method (11)** refactoring (to inline those delegating methods with client code). We can also use **Replace Delegation with Inheritance (20)** to turn middle man into a subclass of the real object.

As martin fowler has mentioned "It's hard to figure out what the right amount of hiding is. Fortunately, with Hide Delegate and Remove Middle Man, it does not matter so much. You can adjust your system as time goes on. As the system changes, the basis for how much you hide also changes. A good encapsulation six months ago may be awkward now. Refactoring means you never have to say you're sorry—you just fix it" [16].

Refactoring – How?
So far we have seen when to perform refactoring and we have discussed some common smells in code…now we will see the explanation of the refactoring techniques (numbered and bold) discussed above. Before starting refactoring we need to ensure that we have a good set of tests to check the result of refactoring, it would be good if we write test before writing the code because in that way we are performing **TDD.** Goal of our tests should be to cover risks not the code coverage!

For the convenience of reading, this list of refactoring techniques is arranged in an alphabetical order:

1. **Collapse Hierarchy-** As the name suggest this refactoring is about collapsing the hierarchy that means we are merging the subclass with superclass, it is possible only when these classes are not very different…it is the opposite of Extract Class and Extract Subclass. To perform this first we need to decide which class will be removed (superclass or subclass), after identifying this we can use **Pull Up Field** and **Pull Up Method** or **Push Down Method** and **Push Down Field** to move all the behavior and data of the removed class to the class with which we have merged it. This reduces the complexity and eases the navigation.

   Side Effect- If the class whose hierarchy we are collapsing has more than one subclasses then remaining subclasses should become inheritors of the class in which hierarchy was collapsed but this can led to the violation of Liskov substitution principle.

2. **Decompose Conditional-** When we have a complicated conditional (if – then- else) statement then we can decompose it by using Extract Method from its 'condition', 'then' and 'else' part (or from where it is possible). If there is a nested conditional then we should decompose each of the conditionals or can try (if it make sense) **Replace Conditional with Guard Clause**. Extracting conditional code into methods makes the code easier to read, understand and maintain.

3. **Duplicate Observed Data-**This refactoring is applicable in a situation when our domain data is available in a class which is responsible for GUI and we want to have multiple interface view of the same data (like desktop app and mobile app) then if we will not separate the domain data from GUI, it will create problem and code duplication. Duplicate Observed Data refactoring split the GUI and domain data into separate objects and setup an observer (using observer design pattern) to synchronize these two…

   To perform this we need to hide direct access to domain data in GUI class (we can use SelfEncapsulatedField), create getter/setter for this data. In the GUI class event handlers we can use setters to set new field values, after this create a domain class and copy necessary fields from GUI class to domain class, create getter/setter, now create an Observer pattern for these two classes.
   This refactoring splits the responsibility of one class into separate classes and maintains SRP (Single Responsibility Principle), for new GUI interface we need not to touch the code logic and vice versa. Now different developers can handle different things and it is easy to maintain domain objects separate from GUI.

4. **Extract Class-** When a class is performing more than one task (violation of SRP), we can use extract class, that is we can create a new class and move relevant information (fields/methods) from old class to new class. This makes code more understandable and manageable. To perform this we create a new class using Extract class refactoring option and

then we can use Move Field and Move Method for those fields and methods that should be placed in new class. And we can also establish some relationship between the old class and new one. Lastly we can consider changing the name of the old class if it is no more remain relevant with the left functionality inside. This refactoring is the inverse of Inline class.

5. **Extract Interface-**We use Extract Interface when multiple classes (clients) are using the subset of a class or part of interface in two classes is the same. Some operations (protocol) that a class performs are common and multiple clients need that, in this situation it is good to create a separate interface for those commonalities so that clients can implement them. Extract Interface may seem similar to Extract Superclass, but we need to remember that extract interface allows isolating common interface not common code, which means if a class is containing some duplicate code, extracting only interface will not remove the duplication, for that we need to use Extract Class, to move the duplicate behavior in a separate component. Extract Interface is also useful in a situation when a class has distinct roles in different situation, then we can use Extract Interface for each role.

6. **Extract Method-** When we have a code fragment that can be grouped together, we can turn that into a method and put a call to this method in place of the code. If a method is too long or if a code needs comment to understand it, then it's time to apply Extract method. This refactoring makes the code easy to understand and we often use this as a step in other refactoring techniques. We need to ensure that the name of the method which we are creating should describe its purpose. Extract Method is the inverse of Inline Method.

7. **Extract superclass/subclass-** When we have more than one class with common field and methods, then using **Extract Superclass**, we can create a shared superclass for them and move all the common behavior inside that superclass. To perform this we create an abstract superclass, and then use Pull Up Field and Pull Up Method to move common data and behavior. This removes duplication but we cannot perform this with the classes that already have a superclass.

   Extract Subclass is applicable on a class that contains some features which are not applicable in all cases, using this we can create a subclass for the subset of those features...now the question comes why can't we use Extract Class for this, we cannot because even though these features are rarely used the class which is containing them is responsible for these features, moving them in a separate unrelated class will shift its responsibility, which is wrong! Therefore it is good to create a subclass for those features.

   To perform this we create a subclass from existing class, and then using push down fields and push down methods we move data and behavior in the new subclass. Both Extract Superclass and Extract Subclass are inverse of Collapse Hierarchy, because here we creating hierarchy in place of collapsing it, but caution need to be taken because hierarchy brings its own complications...

8. **Extract the Loop or Split Loop-** When a loop is performing more than one thing, we can duplicate the loop and separate its responsibilities…It may seem irrational because first thing comes in mind is that when I can perform two task in one iteration then why should I split it? But we need to understand that this splitting is going to optimize our loop which brings clarity and removes temps. To perform this we need to simply copy the loop and separate the different tasks, we can also consider applying Extract Method or Replace Temp with Query (23) on each loop.

9. **Form Template Method-** When our subclasses contain an algorithm whose steps are similar then we can move the algorithm and Its similar steps in superclass and leave the implementation of different steps in the subclasses. This is called Form Template Method refactoring because we are forming a template method in superclass and allowing subclasses to customize it as per their needs. Creating a template method eliminates the duplication by merging the shared algorithm steps in a superclass and leaving just the differences in the subclasses.

   To perform this we can use Extract Method to split algorithm in subclasses and then all identical methods can be moved to a superclass using Pull Up Method. Also move the signatures of non-similar methods to a superclass as abstract and leave their implementation in the subclasses.

10. **Hide Delegate-** Typically in a message chain situation, we expose our delegate object to client, for example client gets object B from a field or method of object A. Then the client calls a method of object B. Through Hide Delegate refactoring we create a new method in class A that delegates the call to object B. Now the client does not know about or depend on class B. To perform this for each method of the delegate-class called by the client, create a method in the server-class that delegates the call to the delegate-class, after that change the client code so that it calls the methods of the server-class. If your changes free the client from needing the delegate-class, you can remove the access method to the delegate-class from the server-class (the method that was originally used to get the delegate-class).

   Hide Delegate's benefits is that it hides delegation from client, because exposing our domain structure to client is not good, and it also create dependency between client and server code's (code which client is directly accessing) structure. But excessive use of this refactoring often turns server class into a Middle Man, a class which delegates half of its client calls to another class…

11. **Inline Class-** If a class is not doing so much work, (maybe it was doing earlier but excessive use of Extract Class has left only few lines of code inside it or maybe because it was planned to be implemented earlier but that need got change, whatever..) then we can move all its features into another class and delete it. Inline class is opposite of Extract Class, eliminating unnecessary classes frees up operating memory and improves bandwidth.

12. **Inline Method-** If a method's body is quite clear and there is no such reason exist to keep its code in named method then we can put the method's body into the body of its callers and delete the method. Inline method is opposite of Extract Method, minimizing the number of unneeded methods makes the code more clear and straightforward.

13. **Introduce parameter Object-** When our methods contain a repeating group of parameters, we can replace these parameters with an object that is called Introduce Parameter Object. By consolidating parameters in a single class, we can also move the methods for handling this data there as well, freeing the other methods from this code.

    To perform this Create a new class that will represent your group of parameters. Make the class immutable. In the method that you want to refactor, use Add Parameter, so that parameter object will get passed. In all method calls, pass the object created from old method parameters to this parameter. Now start deleting old parameters from the method one by one, replacing them in the code with fields of the parameter object. Test the program after each parameter replacement. When done, see whether there is any point in moving a part of the method (or sometimes even the whole method) to a parameter object class. If so, use Move Method or Extract Method. It removes duplication and makes the code more readable.

14. **Move Field-** If a field is used more in another class than its own class (for example optional fields of a class), then create a field in a new class and redirect all users of old field to it. If the field is public we can use Encapsulate field, that is make the field private and provide public access methods. After that create the same field in new class with access methods, replace all references to the old field with appropriate calls to methods in the new class. If the field is not private, take care of this in the superclass and subclasses and finally delete the field in the original class.

15. **Move Method-** If a method is used more in another class than its own class, then create a new method in the class that uses the method the most, move code from the old method to new method. Turn the code of the original method into a reference to the new method in the other class or else remove it entirely. This reduces dependency between classes and makes the class internally more coherent.

16. **Preserve whole object-** Sometimes we fetch several values from an object and then we pass those values as parameter to some method call, Preserve Whole Object says why not pass the whole object! For example :

int value1 = someObject().getFirstValue();
int value2 = someObject().getSecondValue();
obj.useValuesOfSomeObject(value1, value2);

The problem with above code is that each time before our method get called, methods of someObject must be called, if these methods get changed, our task will get complicated because we will need to find all those places where we have made such calls and change them carefully!!
Therefore instead of this we can do this: obj.useValuesOfSomeObject(someObject());

After applying this refactoring the code for getting all necessary data is stored in one place, the methods itself. If the methods needs more data from someObject we can do that easily, and this removes the Long Parameter List (smell) too.

17. **Pull up method/Push Down Method- Pull Up Method** says if our subclasses contains methods that are performing the same work, then their right place is Superclass, so we should make the method identical and move them to the relevant superclass. This removes duplication and if we need to make some changes to this method, we will do that in a single place- the Superclass.

   Push Down Method is the opposite of Pull Up Method, that is if superclass contains a method which is relevant only for some of its subclasses, then move it to those subclasses...this improves class coherence, a method is located where we expect to see it.

18. **Remove Middle Man-** Middle Man is class which is delegating half of its client calls to another class, if a class is doing too much simple delegation then it turns into a middle man.

   Now the question comes when we should think about removing this middle man class? It may require in two scenarios, one is that when this Middle Man class (also called Server for the Client because Client code is directly accessing it) is not doing anything except delegation and second is that when for every new feature in delegate object (the end object) we are creating a delegating method for it in the Middle Man class, if this happened frequently it become tedious, therefore in both the scenarios we need give a thought whether we need this middle man class anymore! If not then simply make the client to call delegate object directly, remove the delegating methods from Server class and put a direct call to delegate object (getters).

19. **Remove Parameter-** It is as simple as its name, when a parameter is no longer used by the method body, then it is better to remove it. Sometime we get crazy when after reading the code again and again we could not figure out what this parameter is doing here…it is always good to clean up code from unnecessary information. But if the method is implemented in different ways in subclasses or in a superclass and this parameter is used in those implementations then leave the parameter as it is.

20. **Replace Delegation with Inheritance-** Delegation is more flexible than Inheritance, but if we are writing many simple delegations for all methods of a single delegate (class) then we can clean our code and simplify our task by using inheritance in place of delegation. To perform this we need to make a subclass of the delegate class, place the current object in a field containing a reference to the delegate object, delete all simple delegation methods and replace all references to the delegate field with references to the current object. But remember if are not using all the methods of the class to which we are delegating, we shouldn't use Replace Delegation with Inheritance.

Sometimes we need to perform another refactoring which is just the opposite of it and that is **Replace Inheritance with Delegation.**

21. **Replace Method with Method Object-** When we have a long method in which the local variables are used in such a way that we cannot perform Extract Method, then we can transform the method into a separate class so that local variables become fields of the class, in this way we can split the method into several methods within the same class. Before applying Replace Method with Method Object we need to give some thought because remember this refactoring will create a new class which may increase overall complexity of the program

22. **Replace Parameter with Method-** The idea behind this refactoring is that if a method can get a value that is passes in as parameter by another means, it should, because long parameter list are difficult to understand, and we should reduce them as much as possible. So if an object is calling a method say x- then passing the result (return value) as a parameter to another method say y, then why can't this receiver method y invoke that method x(inside its body)…remove the parameter and let the receiver invoke the method, this parameter value we can obtained inside the method itself.

Replace Parameter with Method brings clarity in the code and makes code more readable and maintainable.

23. **Replace Temp with Query-** If we are performing some calculations and using temp variables to store the result of an expression, then we can extract that expression into a method and now we can replace expression with a call to this method (which will return the result we were calculating), this new method which we have created can then be used in other methods (if necessary). This refactoring makes the code more readable and removes duplication.

24. **Substitute Algorithm-** Why we will substitute our algorithm, obviously if we have a new and better algorithm (maybe because our requirement has changed) than older one! So it is as simple as that, replace an existing algorithm with the new one.

    To perform this, Make sure that you have simplified the existing algorithm as much as possible, now create your new algorithm in a new method, replace the old algorithm with the new one and start testing the program. When all tests are successfully completed, delete the old algorithm for good!

These are just frequently used refactoring techniques for some common code smells but there are several other refactoring techniques exist and they are equally significant in different scenarios, compiling them in a chapter is not possible. Martin Fowler has written an excellent book which is a detailed (with examples) study of Refactoring, for in depth knowledge of Refactoring I would recommend his book "Refactoring: Improving the Design of Existing Code".

A sound practice and knowledge of good design/bad design brings confidence which is required to apply these techniques, often people debate and talk about reasons of not doing refactoring and give examples when not to perform refactoring, but I would say there maybe some situations in which not touching the working code is a mutual understanding among team but in all other cases cleaning up the code cannot harm anybody!! And as Mr. Kent Beck has said Refactoring is a learnable skills, and to learn it one can follow these 4 tips- Get used to picking a refactoring goal, Stop when you are unsure, Backtrack (in a last good known state) and do it in a pair.

CHAPTER 7

CONTINUOUS INTEGRATION

In this chapter we will discuss Continuous Integration (CI), Continuous Delivery and Continuous Deployment, CI principles, advantages of CI, the deployment pipeline and we will also take a look at the CI best practices for team and the tools that are required to implement CI.

To begin with let me share the definition of CI given by Martin Fowler: A Software Development practice where members of the team integrate their work frequently, leading to multiple integrations per day. Each integration is followed by an automated build including testing to detect Integration problems as quickly as possible [14]. This definition is quite complete in itself; CI is one of the twelve practices of Extreme Programming, it talks about merging development work with a Master/Trunk/Mainline branch frequently so that we can test our changes and can also test that our changes working with other changes or not, this helps in catching the issues (integration) early.

Continuous Delivery is about adopting a software development discipline so that software can be released to production at any time. Once the developer feels the code is ready ship he/she can deliver the code to an environment, this could be UAT or Staging or could be Production. But the idea is that you are delivering code to a user base, whether it is QA or customers for continual review and inspection [15].

The difference between Continuous Integration and Continuous Delivery is that, in continuous delivery process we can perform business logic tests as well because unit tests cannot catch all business logic issues particularly if it is related with design. Moreover we can also deliver our code for Code Review. The basis of Continuous Delivery is small batches of work continually fed to the next step will be consumed more easily and find more issues early on. This system is easier for the developer because issues are presented to the developer before the task has left their memory [15]. Continuous Delivery is achieved when development teams continuously Integrate their software, to do this we use a deployment pipeline (will discuss later). Now let's take a look at another similar word- Continuous Deployment.

Continuous Deployment- Continuous Delivery is sometimes confused with Continuous Deployment. Continuous Deployment means that every change goes through the pipeline and automatically gets put into production, resulting in many production deployments every day. Continuous Delivery just means that you are able to do frequent deployments but may choose not to do it, usually due to businesses preferring a slower rate of deployment. In order to do Continuous Deployment you must be doing Continuous Delivery [17].

In other words Continuous Deployment is the deployment or release of code to Production as soon as it is ready. Any testing is done prior to merging to the Mainline branch and is performed on Production-like environments. The Production branch is always stable and ready to be deployed by an automated process, the automated process should enable anyone to deploy code with just a press of button. After a deploy, logs must be inspected to determine if your key metrics are affected, positively or negatively, some of these metrics may include revenue, user sign-up, response time or traffic etc [15]. So in order to perform Continuous Deployment one should do Continuous Integration and Continuous Delivery first.

Principals of CI:

Now let's take a look at some guiding principles of Continuous Integration, in an ideal CI workflow the entire process should be automated from start to finish.

Single Source Code Repository- Keeping lots of files together to build a product and keeping track of all of these is a huge task but nowadays there are tools to manage all this. Widely used open source repository is Subversion, it is important that teams should put everything in this repository that is required to generate a build (test scripts, properties files, database schema, install scripts, and third party libraries), not just code. We also need to keep the use of branches to minimum, in particular have a mainline: a single branch of the project currently under development.

Automated and Single Command Builds- Automated and single command build tools are quite common these days, like java community has ANT and .NET has NANT and MSBuild. We need to ensure that we build and launch our system using these scripts using a single command.

Dedicated Server for Continuous Integration- It is good have a dedicated build server where we can synchronize and compile the sources and run unit tests. CI server like Bamboo, CruiseControl, Hudson, Continuum etc are really helpful.

Dedicated Infrastructure for Continuous Deployment- Continuous Deployment process needs several pieces of automation in place. One must automate the Continuous Integration Build Server and Continuous Delivery to Staging, as well as should have the ability to automatically deploy to Production.

Continuous Deployment depends on small changes which are constantly tested and those are deployed and released to Production immediately upon verification, automation of steps makes this process simple, consistent and error free.

Martin Fowler has suggested some principles/practices to be followed in order to implement continuous integration, and these are- Maintain a code repository, Automate the build, Make the build self-testing, Everyone commits to the baseline every day, Every commit (to baseline) should be built, Keep the build fast, Test in a clone of the production environment, Make it easy to get the latest deliverables, Everyone can see the results of the latest build and Automate deployment.

You can read his full article at:
http://martinfowler.com/articles/continuousIntegration.html#PracticesOfContinuousIntegration

Advantages of CI:

Reduced Risk- With Continuous Integration we are detecting and fixing defects early (with each integration), and this reduces risks and makes life of everyone a lot more easy.

Increased Visibility- Project state is visible to all, at anytime we can see where our project is, what is working, what is not, the outstanding bugs in system and also running application allow good feedback cycle and brings greater confidence on software.

Improved Efficiency- Automation is the heart of CI, it reduces repetitive, manual and error prone processes and saves people's time (a valuable asset), and this time can be utilized for more value creation.

Increased Availability- With CI one thing is sure- a deployable/working application is available anytime and anyplace.

Concept of Deployment Pipeline: For continuous delivery we can establish a deployment pipeline, it breaks the software delivery process into stages and reduces feedback cycle. A typical CD pipeline includes three stages: **Build automation and continuous integration** (pipeline starts by building binaries that will be passed to other stages, new features are integrated into central code base, build and unit tested), **test automation** (in this stage new version of application is thoroughly tested) and **deployment automation** (deployment is required to test application in an environment, deployment can be staged by releasing new version initially in a production like environment to monitor it before completely rolling out, deployment should be automated for reliable delivery).

Usually the first stage of a deployment pipeline will do any compilation and provide binaries for later stages. Later stages may include manual checks, such as any tests that can't be automated. Stages can be automatic, or require human authorization to proceed, they may be parallelized over many machines to speed up the build. Deploying into production is usually the final stage in a pipeline [18].

Deployment pipeline's main job is to detect any changes that will lead to problems in production. These can include performance, security, or usability issues. A deployment pipeline should enable collaboration between the various groups involved in delivering software and provide everyone visibility about the flow of changes in the system, together with a thorough audit trail [18]. Martin Fowler in his article "Deployment Pipeline" mentioned that a good way to introduce continuous delivery is to model your current delivery process as a deployment pipeline, then examine this for bottlenecks, opportunities for automation, and collaboration points.

Pipeline is supported by platform provisioning and configuration management, which allow team to tear down complete environments automatically or at the push of a button. Multiple stage in deployment pipeline involve different group of people collaborating and supervising release of a new version. Release and pipeline automation provides a top level view of entire pipeline. By **carrying out value stream mappings on your releases**, we can highlight any remaining inefficiencies and hot spots, and pinpoint opportunities to improve our pipeline.

Best Practices for Team: Continuous Integration is a shared practice and certain level of discipline and some good habits can make it more effective.

Commit Code Frequently- It is very first habit that a CI developer should adopt because it is the base of the whole process. For this he/she need to learn how to break down a big work into smaller manageable task units, then should commit after each task instead of waiting till end of the day or some event. Also generally a developer has this tendency for deferring his/her commit till the code become perfect, this tendency needs to get change because we need to commit our code frequently and it would be good if we work on its perfection side after receiving some feedback about it.

Don't commit broken code- This habit is somehow linked with the above one, I have seen some people don't mind committing a broken build…what purpose does it solve? We need to remember that now our code is a shared responsibility and just because you were asked to do it fast; it does not mean that you can escape it without fixing! Always try to make your build script robust and complete and always run private build before committing your changes to version control repository.

Fix Broken Build immediately- A broken build is not just a compilation error, there can be several other reasons for it, and delay in fixing a broken build can lead to multiple problems. The need is to consider it as "our system" and not just the responsibility of the person who has committed something wrong.

Write Automated Tests- Writing tests is important, but for an effective CI it is more important that the tests should be automated and should be a part of automated build process.

All Tests and Inspections Must Pass- One more thing that a CI developer should ensure before committing is that all tests should pass, committing with even a single failed test can harm the whole process.

Avoid Getting Broken Code- When a build is broken avoid taking the latest changes from the central repository, this may lead to integrations issues in your local environment and result in a loss of time to fix the mess.

Don't Commit On an Already Broken Build- Even if you are in a hurry because your shift is about to end, do not commit on an already broken build, in this way we are just adding to the problems, because finding and solving the problem will take a lot of time and energy.

Continuously Monitor and Improve- This is one opportunity that CI brings, anyone can monitor the state of the system and can help to improve it. CI team member should check reports about code quality and other aspects regularly, brings those issues to team meetings, discuss and reach to common census and also identify new areas for improvement continuously.

In a typical CI workflow, Developer checks in code to development branch, Continuous Integration Server picks up the change, performs Unit Tests, votes on the Merge to Staging environment based on test results, if successful deploys it to Staging Environment, QA tests the Environment, if passed, they vote to move to Production, Continuous Integration server picks this up again and determines if it is ok to merge into Production, if successful, it will deploy to Production environment. This process varies slightly based on needs, requirements and approaches [15].

Now take a look at the **Tools required for implementing CI-**

VERSION CONTROL- Open Source- CVS, SVN, GitHub

Commercial- Clear Case

TESTING- Unit Testing Framework- X-Unit, Mocking Framework

Integration Testing Framework- Fitnesse, Selenium

Performance Testing- Load Runner, JMeter

BUILD- Ant, Maven, N-Ant, Scripting

INSPECTION- PMD, Jdepend, Cobertura, Clover, CheckStyle, Emma, FindBugs, JavaNCCS

CONTINUOUS INTEGRATION SERVER- Bamboo, CruiseControl, Hudson, Continuum, Anthill

A more detail description of tools is given in the next chapter- tools for agile development

CHAPTER **8**

TOOLS for AGILE DEVELOPMENT

In this chapter will take a look at some popular tools/frameworks which an agile team member should use.

TDD Toolkit- For Java Projects-:

JUnit- Java Test Framework, JUnit is the Java version of the xUnit architecture for unit- and regression-testing frameworks. Written by Erich Gamma and Kent Beck, it's distributed as an open source project, includes the core test framework class hierarchy, and defines a common language for writing and running repeatable tests. JUnit uses reflection to examine the tests and code under tests. This allows JUnit to execute any method of any class and examine the results. Many IDEs have built-in support for JUnit.

http://junit.org/

HttpUnit- Written by Russell Gold, is an open source Java library for black-box testing HTTP-based Web applications and servlets. The library supports testing applications containing the following: Basic and form-based authentication, State management with cookies, JavaScript and Automatic page redirection. HttpUnit easily integrates with JUnit for fast development of HTTP-based functional tests. It also contains a servlet test framework, ServletUnit, which can be used to help develop servlets. Written in Java, HttpUnit allows Java test code to process returned pages as text, XML DOM, or containers of forms, tables and links.

http://httpunit.sourceforge.net/

Ant- A cross-platform build and scripting tool, it was developed as a Java and XML-based open source project by the Apache Software Foundation. Ant supplies a number of built-in tasks allowing to compile, assemble, test and run Java applications. Ant is written in Java and can easily be extended to create custom tasks whenever necessary also it is extremely flexible and does not impose coding conventions or directory layouts to the Java projects which adopt it as a build tool. A default Ant install supports a number of Java-specific tasks plus many platform-independent file management tasks for automating the entire build process.

http://ant.apache.org/

plus **Refactoring IDE like JDeveloper, IntelliJ IDEA, NetBeans and Eclipse**

For .NET Projects-

NUnit- NUnit is an open source unit testing framework for Microsoft .NET. It serves the same purpose as JUnit does in the Java world, and is one of many programs in the xUnit family.

http://www.nunit.org/

xUnit.Net- A free, open source, community-focused unit testing tool for the .NET Framework. Written by the original inventor of NUnit v2, xUnit.net is the latest technology for unit testing C#, F#, VB.NET and other .NET languages. xUnit.net works with ReSharper, CodeRush, TestDriven.NET and Xamarin.

https://xunit.github.io/

mbUnit- The Gallio Automation Platform is an open, extensible, and neutral system for .NET that provides a common object model, runtime services and tools (such as test runners) that may be leveraged by any number of test frameworks. MbUnit is an extensible unit testing framework for the .NET Framework that takes in and goes beyond xUnit pattern testing. MbUnit is part of the Gallio bundle. It has good support for RowTests.

https://code.google.com/p/mb-unit/

NAnt- NAnt is a free and open source software tool for automating software build processes. It is similar to Apache Ant, but targeted at the .NET environment rather than Java. The name NAnt comes from the fact that the tool is Not Ant.

http://nant.sourceforge.net/

and **popular Visual Studio Code Refactoring Tools are: JustCode, ReSharper by JetBrains, CodeRush, Visual Assist X, VSCommands for Visual Studio 2012 and DPack**

CI Toolkit- For Version Control:

CVS - The Concurrent Versions System (CVS), also known as the Concurrent Versioning System, is a open source client-server software revision control system. Dick Grune developed CVS as a series of shell scripts in July 1986. Tortoise CVS is a great client for CVS on Windows, and there are many different IDEs, such as Xcode (Mac), Eclipse, NetBeans and Emacs, that use CVS.

http://www.nongnu.org/cvs/

Subversion (SVN) - Apache subversion (SVN), is one of most popular software versioning and revision control system distributed as open source software. Software developers use Subversion to maintain current and historical versions of files such as source code, web pages, and documentation. Many different Subversion clients are available for Windows user- Tortoise SVN for Mac- Versions is an elegant client and Xcode is Apple's developer environment and Subversion client.

https://subversion.apache.org/

Git- It is a distributed revision control system with an emphasis on speed, data integrity, and support for distributed, non-linear workflows. Git was initially designed and developed by Linus Torvalds for Linux kernel development in 2005. Git offers a much different type of version control in that it's a distributed version control system. With a distributed version control system, there isn't one centralized code base to pull the code from. Different branches hold different parts of the code.

https://git-scm.com/

Mercurial- Mercurial is a cross-platform, distributed revision control tool, it is mainly implemented using the Python programming language, but includes a binary diff implementation written in C. It is supported on MS Windows and Unix-like systems, such as FreeBSD, Mac OS X and Linux. Mercurial is primarily a command line program but graphical user interface extensions are available.

https://www.mercurial-scm.org/

Other version control systems are: **Bazaar** - http://bazaar.canonical.com/en/ , **LibreSource** - http://dev.libresource.org/ and **Monotone-** http://monotone.ca/

TESTING- Unit Testing – X unit and Mocking Frameworks (Unit Testing frameworks for Java and .NET discussed above)

Integration Testing:

Fitnesse- FitNesse is a web server, a wiki and an automated testing tool for software. It is based on Ward Cunningham's Framework for Integrated Test and is designed to support acceptance testing rather than unit testing in that it facilitates detailed readable description of system function. FitNesse allows users of a developed system to enter specially formatted input (its format is accessible to non-programmers). This input is interpreted and tests are created automatically. These tests are then executed by the system and output is returned to the user. The advantage of this approach is very fast feedback from users. FitNesse is written in Java (by Robert C. Martin and others). The program first supported only Java, but versions for several other languages have been added over time (C++, Python, Ruby, Delphi, C#, etc.).

http://www.fitnesse.org/

Selenium- Selenium is a portable software testing framework for web applications. Selenium provides a record/playback tool for authoring tests without learning a test scripting language (Selenium IDE). It also provides a test domain-specific language (Selenese) to write tests in a number of popular programming languages, including Java, C#, Groovy, Perl, PHP, Python and Ruby. The tests can then be run against most modern web browsers. Selenium deploys on Windows, Linux, and Macintosh platforms. It is open-source software, released under the Apache 2.0 license, and can be downloaded and used without charge.

http://www.seleniumhq.org/

Performance Testing:

Load Runner- HP LoadRunner is a software testing tool from Hewlett-Packard. It is used to test applications, measuring system behaviour and performance under load. HP acquired LoadRunner as part of its acquisition of Mercury Interactive in November 2006. HP LoadRunner can simulate thousands of users concurrently using application software, recording and later analysing the performance of key components of the application. LoadRunner simulates user activity by generating messages between application components or by simulating interactions with the user interface such as keypresses or mouse movements. The messages/interactions to be generated are stored in scripts. LoadRunner can generate the scripts by recording them, such as logging HTTP requests between a client web browser and an application's web server.

http://www8.hp.com/in/en/software-solutions/loadrunner-load-testing/

JMeter- Apache JMeter may be used to test performance both on static and dynamic resources (Webservices (SOAP/REST), Web dynamic languages - PHP, Java, ASP.NET, Files, etc. -, Java Objects, Data Bases and Queries, FTP Servers and more). It can be used to simulate a heavy load on a server, group of servers, network or object to test its strength or to analyze overall performance under different load types. You can use it to make a graphical analysis of performance or to test your server/script/object behavior under heavy concurrent load.

http://jmeter.apache.org/

BUILD- Ant, Maven, nAnt and Scripting

CONTINUOUS INTEGRATION SERVER:

CruiseControl- A Java-based framework for a continuous build process, It includes dozens of plugins for a variety of source controls, build technologies, and notifications schemes including email and instant messaging. A web interface provides details of the current and previous builds. CruiseControl is written in Java but is used on a wide variety of projects. There are builders supplied for Ant, NAnt, Maven, Phing, Rake, and Xcode, and the catch-all exec builder that can be used with any command-line tool or script. It was originally developed by employees at ThoughtWorks, but is now an independent project.

http://cruisecontrol.sourceforge.net/

CruiseControl.NET- an Automated Continuous Integration server, implemented using the .NET Framework.

And many other CI servers are popular like:

Anthill: Now distributed by IBM and implemented in Java. It has a proprietary license.

Bamboo: Atlassian's CI server isn't open source, but the Java code is provided to customers for free. It is also free for open source and community projects to use.

Buildbot: An open source offering - Brian Warner's Python based CI tool.

Continuum: An Apache build tool developed in Java.

easyCIS: Freeware CI server developed by Václav Zahradník on top of the .NET framework.

FinalBuilder Server/Continua CI: CI server from VSoft written in C#.

Go: ThoughtWorks' continuous delivery tool written in Java.

Gump: The Apache Software Foundation's first CI tool. Written in Python it supports Apache Ant and Maven, amongst others.

Hudson: Java CI server now managed by the Eclipse Foundation.

Jenkins: An open source tool written in Java. The project was forked from Hudson after a dispute with Oracle and is now led by CloudBees.

Mojo: OpenMake's free Java-based CI server.

Parabuild: Java-based server from Viewtier Systems.

Pulse: Java-based CI server from Zutubi.

QuickBuild: PMEase's Java-based CI tool.

Sin: CI tool written in C# by Casper Hornstrup. It supports Subversion and is licensed with GPL.

TeamCity: Java-based CI server from JetBrains, makers of IntelliJ.

Team Foundation Server: Microsoft's CI sever, widely used by .NET developers.

TravisCI: Hosted continuous integration service for the open source community.

Zed: Java-based CI Server from Hericus Software.

(source: http://www.infoq.com/research/ci-server)

TOOLS FOR INSPECTION- PMD, Jdepend, Cobertura, Clover, CheckStyle, Emma, FindBugs, JavaNCCS

A Brief Introduction to BDD- Behavior-Driven Development (BDD) is an agile process that is designed to keep the focus on stakeholder value throughout the whole project. The main concept of BDD is that the requirement has to be written in a way that everyone understands it – business representative, analyst, developer, tester, manager, etc. A BDD story is written by the whole team and used as both requirements and executable test cases. It is a way to perform test-driven development (TDD) but combines ideas from Domain Driven Design and Object Oriented Analysis and Design, it provides Shared tools/Shared process for collaboration. In other words it is a way to describe and test functionality in (almost) natural language.

BDD Story Format: Even though there are different variations of the BDD story template, they all have two common elements: narrative and scenario. Each narrative is followed by one or more scenarios.

The BDD story format looks like this:

Narrative:

In order to [benefit]

As a [role]

I want to [feature]

Scenario: [description]

Given [context or precondition]

When [event or action]

Then [outcome validation]

BDD Tools:

For Java- JBehave- JBehave is a framework for Behaviour-Driven Development (BDD). BDD is an evolution of test-driven development (TDD) and acceptance-test driven design, and is intended to make these practices more accessible and intuitive to newcomers and experts alike.

http://jbehave.org/

For .NET- SpecFlow- SpecFlow is open source and provided under a BSD license. As a part of the Cucumber family, SpecFlow uses the official Gherkin parser and provides integration to the .NET framework, Silverlight, Windows Phone and Mono.

http://www.specflow.org/

Other BDD tools are **NSpec, Cucumber, RSpec, Jasmine, JDave, Concordion and Easyb**

Mocking Frameworks-

For Java- Mockito- http://mockito.org/

       EasyMock- http://easymock.org/

       PowerMock- https://github.com/jayway/powermock

For .NET- FakeItEasy- https://github.com/FakeItEasy/FakeItEasy

       Moq- https://github.com/Moq/moq4

       NSubstitute- https://github.com/nsubstitute/NSubstitute

       Rhino Mocks- https://github.com/RhinoMocks/RhinoMocks

       NMock3- https://nmock3.codeplex.com/

And now some Tools for Agile project management-

JIRA- A proprietary issue tracking product, developed by Atlassian. It provides bug tracking, issue tracking, and project management functions.

https://www.atlassian.com/software/jira

VersionOne- VersionOne is an all-in-one enterprise agile solution for software organizations scaling agile. From discovery to delivery, VersionOne scales to any number of organizational levels and supports methodologies such as the Scaled Agile Framework, Enterprise Scrum, Kanban, DAD, LeSS, or a Hybrid approach.

https://www.versionone.com/

Rally- Rally is recently purchased by CA Technologies, it offers different products like: Rally Unlimited Edition, Rally Team Start, Flowdock and Rally Insights Analytics which are quite popular.

Some other popular agile project management tools are:

ActiveCollab- https://www.activecollab.com/

AgileBench- https://agilebench.com/

Agilo for Scrum- http://www.agilosoftware.com/

Pivotal Tracker- http://www.pivotaltracker.com/

Telerik TeamPulse- http://www.telerik.com/teampulse

Additional Views: Next four chapters are some of my views on latest happenings/trends related with Scrum/Agile….

CHAPTER 9

WATERFALL TO AGILE

I have read the agile transformation stories of some big organizations. I have also observed that even though the strategic management (through media and annual conference messages) delivers its vision of moving toward agility and its emphasis that it is the need of the hour, still, some of these organizations are not successful in their adoption and implementation. These organizations have run their pilot projects and programs, but after documenting the lessons learned or presenting a white paper on their implementation journey, they are still handling development by using Waterfall. Here I would like to share what I believe can be an approach toward implementation of Scrum/Agile [19].

In my view, there can be two possible ways to implement Scrum/Agile at the team level.

Traditional approach

The first way of trying implementation is traditional. In this approach:

We introduce Scrum/Agile to teams through training or certification, which is sponsored by the company.

Then we try to encourage the trained members through different activities so that they adopt this culture.

I have seen organizations that have followed this approach and are still using Waterfall, because the process is too traditional. Everyone handles it just like any other training program sponsored by the company. As a result, this process doesn't involve people in the transformation process and doesn't create self-motivated teams.

This led me to think about a second approach, which is a little tricky but quite result-oriented.

Result-oriented approach

In this approach we introduce Scrum/Agile to teams through training or certification, which is conditionally sponsored by the company.

First we make the training mandatory for all team members, and all team members are supposed to pay for this training.

After training, a transition period of one month will start. During this period the trained team members will participate in weekly gatherings/meetings (in the office). In these gatherings they will share their ideas about how they are going to implement the Scrum/Agile framework in their existing and ongoing projects. If these team members show active participation in all these activities, then their training fees will be reimbursed.

Reasons: For the successful implementation of any method, there should be a positive mind-set toward its implementation. Here I would like to mention that, based on my experience, I have generally seen people to have a less-than-serious approach toward company-sponsored training and certification programs. They have different excuses for this:

Because training is free, usually they do not take it seriously.

During the process of adoption, if they face even a small difficulty, they start criticizing the process by saying it isn't effective, the old process was better, the new one is not a good fit for the organizational environment, the new process adds complexity, etc.

I believe the implementation of Agile should be Agile in nature, and through timeboxed, small steps we can achieve this. This second approach may seem difficult to adopt, but I believe it would help us create an atmosphere of interaction/collaboration within the organization. When people gather and think about how they can do something in a more Agile manner in their current project, they will naturally get involved and will start practicing it then and there.

Today a market opportunity comes and goes very quickly, and it is not feasible to run a three-to-four-year Agile transformation program. I have observed that generally the middle management tends to resist Agile/Scrum implementation because of fear of losing control or because they are too comfortable with the existing process and the authority attached to it. The shift from old processes to a new framework is painful, but when brands like Yahoo and Microsoft are taking major steps toward Agile implementation and getting rid of their age-old Waterfall models, do we still need to analyze whether we should adopt Agile/Scrum at our organizations?

Scrum/Agile has an inherent element of customization. This does not mean making changes in the fundamental framework, but it does mean adjusting existing processes to fit and to make people feel comfortable about it.

CHAPTER 10

SCRUM Versus SAFe

I have observed that Scrum focuses on working culture, self-motivation, and mind-set change to bring the best results. A few months back I explored SAFe and found that it is a good recipe for business under the name of Agile. Over time, I have seen that whenever any organization thinks about using a new framework and top management communicated this message to middle management, middle management then becomes the key player in its implementation [20].

The approach of middle management in Scrum implementation

In organizations undergoing Scrum implementation, middle management realizes that in Scrum there is less scope for managerial authority, because Scrum talks about self-motivation and a change in working culture. At that point some middle managers start deteriorating the implementation process and convey the message to top management that this new framework is not a good fit for the organization.

The approach of middle management in SAFe implementation

Here I would like to appreciate the creators of SAFe, because their approach is quite smart. Well aware of this real pain point for middle management in the process of Scrum/Agile implementation, they prepared a recipe that contains management/reporting authority. This is part of the SAFe framework, in the same way that it was in Waterfall and other traditional approaches. This is a reason why middle management tends to feel safe with SAFe. This works well for certain other kinds of people also, for example:

- Those who raise this question in the introduction session of Scrum/Agile trainings: "Where we stand in this framework?"

- Those who believe that only years of experience matter, having no faith in self-education and upgrading.

- Developers who are not happy with the additional tasks Scrum brings them.

- Those who have become isolated in their organization because with Scrum, some younger person is teaching them their job.

Now with SAFe, all these people feeling more engaged because, without too much headache, they can carry on with their familiar positions and levels of authority.

The atmosphere we are witnessing now has been created after a long period of effort within the Scrum community. Now when organizations have started thinking seriously about mind-set and working culture change, SAFe has provided a safe road through which to travel through the business market created by Scrum.

There are proponents of the SAFe framework who say that Scrum has no scope to scale at the enterprise level, and to those I want to say that this is not a well-considered critique. Every individual in an organization should follow an approach that helps them in work smart instead of dragging them back to the Waterfall tradition. This is my observation, because I've been trained and certified in different methods and technologies, and I've found that Scrum/Agile makes you smart. To decide between Scrum and SAFe, organizations need to compare the benefits of each approach, and top management needs to ensure that the comparisons remain unbiased and logical. I believe that Lean, Kanban, and other principles that SAFe claims it contains are already part of the fundamental themes of Scrum; only the terminology is missing, because it is not necessary to include specific terms for the sake of marketing.

CHAPTER 11

CURRENT STATE of AGILE/SCRUM ACCEPTANCE

Some organizations are searching professionals with job offers like agile coach, agile consultant, technical agile coach, TDD and XP agile coach, agilest etc. and some communities are organizing events like agile marathon, agile Olympiad, agile coffee talk, agile tour, agile carnival, scrum/agile gatherings and meet up etc. As we can see all such kind of things are related with Scrum/Agile implementation.

In my view Scrum is good for software development and easy to adopt as well. Earlier different models were in use like waterfall, prototyping, iterative and incremental development, spiral development, rapid application development etc. But hype about agile which is there in the market we have seen never before. I use to explore different technologies/methodologies/frameworks and I found that Scrum is quite developer friendly and looks good at very first glance. There is a possibility that management may not like it because it affects management authority to some extent.

These days Agile is a hot area. What is a typical approach of introducing any framework? First step is training of people who are going to use it and then people start using it. Professionals in software development organization are smart enough to adapt any framework as they are use to of it. The question comes when these people are capable of developing complex systems then why they will not understand a simple framework?

Agile related job profiles which are in trend these days, does not exist in Scrum framework as we all know that Scrum talks about three roles- Scrum Master, Product Owner and Development Team. The scrum master is responsible for all coaching/mentoring related activities for team and for organization in scrum adoption.

Role of Agile Coach- In my view role of agile coach is a byproduct of business and marketing tactics. Those who are involved in its marketing give different excuses for this like it is required for large scale implementation, for complete transformation etc. These things are irrelevant as agile says inspect and adapt.

To conclude, acceptance of Scrum/Agile is quite visible- top brands have accepted it; it is included in academic syllabus and it is now considered as proven successful framework. But at the same time some people are talking about things like TDD is dead, agile is dead: the angry developer version, scrum is dead, The End of Agile: Death by Over Simplification and agile death march etc. this resistance is emerging because of its marketing hype which is a natural process. Change is inevitable and this framework which we are using now will further get improved and introduce with a new name [21]

CHAPTER 12

DevOps

I observed that DevOps approach is a natural part of tech startups culture because startup team consists of few developers who are responsible for full delivery which includes responsibility of operation as well.

What is DevOps: DevOps is an approach which combines development and operations, it emphasize on communication, collaboration and integration between software developers and IT professionals. DevOps improves deployment frequency, which can lead to faster time to market, lower failure rate of new releases, shortened lead time between fixes and faster mean time to recovery in the event of a new release crashing or otherwise disabling the current system, it aims to maximize the predictability, efficiency, security and maintainability of operational processes.

Agile gives organizations the ability to quickly respond in a fast changing market. Here I would like to quote Martin Fowler's definition of DevOps and Continuous Delivery. As Martin Fowler has described that continuous Delivery is a software development discipline where you build software in such a way that the software can be released to production at any time, you achieve continuous delivery by continuously integrating the software done by the development team, building executables and running automated tests on those executables to detect problems. Furthermore you push the executables into increasingly production-like environments to ensure the software will work in production. To achieve continuous delivery you need: a close, collaborative working relationship between everyone involved in delivery (often referred to as a "DevOps culture") and extensive automation of all possible parts of the delivery process, usually using a DeploymentPipeline.

According to puppet labs state of DevOps survey, companies that incorporate DevOps deploy code up to 30 times more frequently than their competitors and less than 50% of their deployments fail. In a typical DevOps environment, there is one team composed of cross-functional team members including developers, QA, DBAs, business analysts, operations engineers and so forth, collaboration across these different roles delivers many benefits.

Technical benefits: continuous software delivery, less complex problems to fix, faster resolution of problems

Business benefits: faster delivery of features, more stable operating environments, more time available to add value (rather than fix/maintain)

The combination of a shared code base, continuous integration, test-driven techniques and automated deploys expose problems in application code, infrastructure or configuration earlier because the software isn't "thrown over the wall" to Operations at the end of coding. Problems tend to be less complex because change sets are smaller. And resolution times are faster because team members don't need to wait for a different team to troubleshoot and fix the problem. DevOps aids in software application release management for an organization by standardizing development environments. Events can be more easily tracked as well as resolving documented process control and granular reporting issues. From methodologies such as Agile, lean principles and just in time manufacturing, startups adopted DevOps as a means to compete, innovate, and move faster. DevOps is inherently a quicker, better way to get product to market – a perfect fit for startups.

Implementing DevOps process usually starts with adopting an automation platform like Chef or Puppet. Once an automation platform has been adopted, it is used to code all systems related configuration and deployment. The idea is to remove the human element of manually configuring servers or deploying an application across multiple environments and multiple servers, automated configuration can get deployed on Cloud-based systems. As per the study of market research firm Gartner there are strong growth opportunities for DevOps toolsets, with the total for DevOps tools reaching $2.3 billion in 2015, up 21.1% from $1.9 billion in 2014. Cloud Providers and their Platform as a Service (PaaS) offering are helping startups and developers with no dedicated Ops team. For startups and tech companies the value of implementing DevOps helps in achieving higher productivity at lower costs resulting in more reliable systems.

Let's take a look at some popular tools which help in the implementation of DevOps, particularly useful for startups…

DevOps Tools:

IBM Bluemix: Bluemix is a cloud platform as a service (PaaS) developed by IBM. It supports several programming languages and services as well as integrated DevOps to build, run, deploy and manage applications on the cloud. Bluemix is based on Cloud Foundry open technology and runs on SoftLayer infrastructure. Bluemix supports several programming languages including Java, Node.js, Go, PHP, Python, Ruby Sinatra, Ruby on Rails and can be extended to support other languages such as Scala through the use of buildpacks.

Atlas: Mitchell Hashimoto's HashiCorp introduced Atlas, an application development and delivery system, it is a unified dashboard and workflow for developing, deploying, and maintaining applications on any public, private, or hybrid infrastructure. It provides visibility into infrastructure, including servers, containers, and virtual machines, in addition to configuration management and service discovery. Atlas enables devops across a variety of cloud services, including AWS, Google Compute Engine, Azure, and OpenStack, and provides a dashboard for developing, deploying, and maintaining applications.

Chef: Chef is a configuration management tool written in Ruby and Erlang. It uses a pure-Ruby, domain-specific language (DSL) for writing system configuration "recipes". Chef is used to streamline the task of configuring and maintaining a company's servers, and can integrate with cloud-based platforms such as Rackspace, Internap, Amazon EC2, Google Cloud Platform, OpenStack, SoftLayer, and Microsoft Azure to automatically provision and configure new machines. Chef contains solutions for both small and large scale systems, with features and pricing for the respective ranges.

Docker: Docker is an open platform for distributed applications, it brings portability to applications via its containerization technology, wherein applications run in self-contained units that can be moved across platforms. It consists of Docker Engine, which is a lightweight runtime and packaging tool, and Docker Hub, a cloud service for application-sharing and workflow automation.

Puppet: Puppet is an open source configuration management utility. It runs on many Unix-like systems as well as on Microsoft Windows, and includes its own declarative language to describe system configuration. Puppet is produced by Puppet Labs, founded by Luke Kanies in 2005. Puppet is designed to manage the configuration of Unix-like and Microsoft Windows systems declaratively. The user describes system resources and their state, either using Puppet's declarative language or a Ruby DSL (domain-specific language). This information is stored in files called "Puppet manifests". Puppet discovers the system information via a utility called Facter and compiles the Puppet manifests into a system-specific catalog containing resources and resource dependency, which are applied against the target systems. Any actions taken by Puppet are then reported.

SaltStack: SaltStack is fast and scalable systems and configuration management software for predictive orchestration, cloud and data center automation, server provisioning, application deployment and more. SaltStack provides systems management for data automation, server provisioning, cloud building, and application configuration. It is an event-driven cloud infrastructure automation tool, it can automate tasks within the devops workflow. SaltStack provides a common way and a common language to manage servers, thereby helping to bridge the gap between the two camps.

ScriptRock GuardRail: GuardRail provides configuration monitoring, with continuous overseeing of machine configuration state. It can help users ensure their production environment is identical to QA, test, and dev environments. ScriptRock's GuardRail is designed to quickly pinpoint differences in configurations on servers and desktops, comparing states between systems and over time. With GuardRail you can see just what has changed, helping simplify diagnostics — and reducing downtime.

Splunk: Splunk is a tool for finding and fixing issues in real time across the application lifecycle, allowing developers to visualize data from production environments without having to access production machines. Splunk helps users embrace devops processes, including continuous integration and deployment.

Recent Developments: On April 15th ProfitBricks, an IaaS provider announced that ProfitBricks will be launching a new DevOps Central and REST API, in combination with API features which are already in place. ProfitBricks is also introducing several new libraries that will greatly increase developers' freedom to choose their own coding language, thus making it easier to integrate ProfitBricks' services into a wider variety of existing networks. The new libraries support Python, Ruby and Java. The Chef company at its recent ChefConf event announced that it is going to launch Chef Delivery, a workflow engine that takes either infrastructure or application code and moves it from the developer's workstation through build, test and production, streamlining software and infrastructure deployment according to patterns that the company has observed at successful DevOps shops. On 22nd April, 2015 Ness Software Engineering

Services (SES), a leading provider of software product engineering services, has announced the launch of its end-to-end, Ness Connected Framework to enhance DevOps on complex projects [22].

References

[1] J. Sutherland, "History: Scrum Guides," 2013. [Online]. Available: http://scrumguides.org/history.html. [Accessed November 2015].

[2] M. Cohn, "Scrum Overview for Agile Software Develpment:mountaingoatsoftware.com," [Online]. Available: https://www.mountaingoatsoftware.com/agile/scrum/overview. [Accessed November 2015].

[3] "https://en.wikipedia.org/wiki/Scrum_(software_development)#Product_increment," [Online]. Available: https://en.wikipedia.org/wiki/Scrum_(software_development)#Product_increment.

[4] M. Cohn, "Multiple Level of Done: Mountaingoat software," 17 Feb 2015. [Online]. Available: https://www.mountaingoatsoftware.com/blog/multiple-levels-of-done. [Accessed November 2015].

[5] D. Leffingwell, "New Principles of Agile Architecture: Scaled Agile Framework," [Online]. Available: http://www.scaledagileframework.com/new-principles-of-agile-architecture/. [Accessed November 2015].

[6] S. W. Ambler, "The Architecture Owner Role: How Architects Fit in on Agile Teams: Agile Modeling.com," [Online]. Available: http://www.agilemodeling.com/essays/architectureOwner.htm. [Accessed November 2015].

[7] S. W. Ambler, "An Introduction to Agile Modeling," [Online]. Available: http://www.agilemodeling.com/essays/introductionToAM.htm. [Accessed November 2015].

[8] M. Fowler, "Test Driven Development," 5 March 2005. [Online]. Available: http://martinfowler.com/bliki/TestDrivenDevelopment.html. [Accessed November 2015].

[9] "BDD: wikipedia.org," [Online]. Available: https://en.wikipedia.org/wiki/Behavior-driven_development. [Accessed November 2015].

[10] D. H. Hansson, "TDD is dead. Long Live Testing," 23 April 2014. [Online]. Available: http://david.heinemeierhansson.com/2014/tdd-is-dead-long-live-testing.html. [Accessed November 2015].

[11] D. H. Hansson, "Test induced Design Damage," 29 April 2014. [Online]. Available: http://david.heinemeierhansson.com/2014/test-induced-design-damage.html. [Accessed November 2015].

[12] "INVEST (mnemonic): Wikipedia," [Online]. Available: https://en.wikipedia.org/wiki/INVEST_(mnemonic).

[13] M. Fowler, "PairProgrammingMisconceptions:martinfowler.com," 31 October 2006. [Online]. Available: http://martinfowler.com/bliki/PairProgrammingMisconceptions.html. [Accessed November 2015].

[14] M. Fowler, "Continuous Integration: martinfowler.com," 1 May 2006. [Online]. Available: http://www.martinfowler.com/articles/continuousIntegration.html. [Accessed November 2015].

[15] M. Chletsos, "Continuous Delivery vs Continuous Deployment vs Continuous Intergration:assembla.com," 29 November 2012. [Online]. Available: http://blog.assembla.com/AssemblaBlog/tabid/12618/bid/92411/Continuous-Delivery-vs-Continuous-Deployment-vs-Continuous-Integration-Wait-huh.aspx. [Accessed November 2015].

[16] M. Fowler, Refactoring: Improving the Design of Existing Code, ADDISON–WESLEY, 1999.

[17] M. Fowler, "Continuous Delivery: martinfowler.com," 30 May 2013. [Online]. Available: http://martinfowler.com/bliki/ContinuousDelivery.html. [Accessed November 2015].

[18] M. Fowler, "Deployment Pipeline: Martin Fowler.com," 30 May 2013. [Online]. Available: http://martinfowler.com/bliki/DeploymentPipeline.html. [Accessed November 2015].

[19] D. Mishra, "Waterfall to Agile: Scrum Alliance Inc.," 7 October 2014. [Online]. Available: https://www.scrumalliance.org/community/articles/2014/october/waterfall-to-agile-%E2%80%93-a-result-oriented-approach.

[20] D. Mishra, "Scrum Versus SAFe," 11 November 2014. [Online]. Available: https://www.scrumalliance.org/community/articles/2014/november/scrum-versus-safe.

[21] D. Mishra, "Current State Of Agile/Scrum Acceptance: a2zstartup.com," 12 October 2015. [Online]. Available: http://www.a2zstartup.com/current-state-of-agilescrum-acceptance/.

[22] D. Mishra, "DevOps," 22 April 2015. [Online]. Available: http://www.a2zstartup.com/devops/.

About the Author: Devsena Mishra is a Certified Scrum Developer, Certified Scrum Product Owner, Certified Scrum Master, Six Sigma Black Belt, Lean Certified, PRINCE2 practitioner and ITIL certified with experience in software development, project/quality management & professional training. She has also earned some 29 international certificates in different technologies (Java/Oracle/Microsoft/SAS).

She has also launched an information portal for startups in India: http://www.a2zstartup.com/

www.ingramcontent.com/pod-product-compliance
Lightning Source LLC
Chambersburg PA
CBHW061037050326
40689CB00012B/2867